Contents

Meet the alien

You probably have a friend or someone in your family who is always asking questions, such as:

Why does this happen?

What makes it do that?

How many are there?

In fact, that person might even be you. The one who is doing all the asking in this book isn't a person at all. It is an alien from outer space.

This particular alien likes asking questions about everything, but won't answer many questions about itself.

We don't know whether the alien is a he or a she, or which planet it comes from. What we do know is its name . . . but it is very long and difficult to spell using any of Earth's languages. We also know that it is very friendly and interested in the planet Earth and what goes on here.

Why don't fish have fingers?

Philip Ardagh

 Belitha Press

First published in Great Britain in 1996 by

Belitha Press Ltd
London House, Great Eastern Wharf
Parkgate Road, London SW11 4NQ

Reprinted in 1997

Editor: Maria O'Neill
Designers: Guy Callaby and Helen James
Picture Researcher: Juliet Duff
Consultant: Steve Parker

ISBN 1 85561 541 X (Hardback)
ISBN 1 85561 593 2 (Paperback)

Printed in Italy

British Library Cataloguing in Publication Data for this book is
available from the British Library.

Photographic credits: J.C. Allen/FLPA 6br. Jane Burton/Bruce
Coleman Ltd /14tr. B.B.Casals/FLPA 17c. David Cayless/OSF 26c.
Martin Colbeck/OSF 13b. Stephen Dalton/NHPA 8c, 24c. Nigel
Dennis/NHPA 12b. Xavier Eichaker/Still Pictures 18c. Dennis
Green/Survival/OSF 19t. Daniel Heuclin/NHPA 23c. E & D
Hosking/FLPA 7tr. G. Moon/FLPA 16b.
R. Oggioni/Panda/FLPA 28b. OSF cover, 10b, 22c. Stan Osolmiski/OSF
20. Richard Packwood/OSF 27t. Fritz Polking/FLPA 29bl. John
Shaw/NHPA 27bl. Claude Steelman/Survival/OSF 9b. Charles
Tyler/OSF 22cr. Barrie Watts/OSF 15t. Christian Weiss/Still Pictures
11. Martin Withers/FLPA 8bl, 16c. Belinda Wright/OSF 21b.

Illustration credits:
All illustrations by Pond and Giles/Wildlife Art Agency
Aliens by Graham Rosewarne

In this book, we answer the alien's questions about Earth's wildlife, in other words, questions about the animals and plants around us.

Perhaps the answers in this book will answer some of your own questions about the creatures that share our planet. Some might set you off on your own investigations.

The Alien

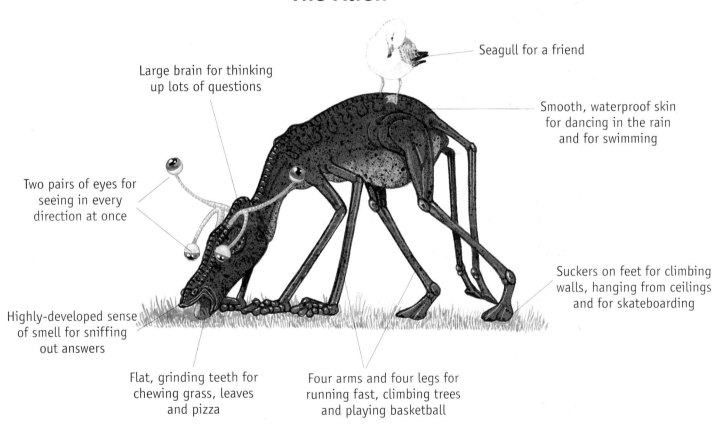

Seagull for a friend

Large brain for thinking up lots of questions

Smooth, waterproof skin for dancing in the rain and for swimming

Two pairs of eyes for seeing in every direction at once

Suckers on feet for climbing walls, hanging from ceilings and for skateboarding

Highly-developed sense of smell for sniffing out answers

Flat, grinding teeth for chewing grass, leaves and pizza

Four arms and four legs for running fast, climbing trees and playing basketball

Some of the more difficult words in this book are printed in **bold** when they first appear. This shows that they are explained in the glossary on page 31.

Why don't plants need noses?

Because animals use their noses to breath in air, which contains oxygen. Plants take in all the oxygen they need to respire (breathe) through their leaves. Plants need oxygen, just like humans do, to keep them alive.

Do they have mouths?

No. Plants usually make their own food, taking what they need from sunshine and soil. Their roots collect water, and their leaves absorb **carbon dioxide** from the air. Most plants use the energy in the Sun's light rays to turn this water and **gas** into a sugary food. This process is called **photosynthesis**.

PHOTOSYNTHESIS AT WORK

1 The rain dampens the soil.

2 The roots of the plant draw up the water from the soil.

3 The leaves **absorb** the carbon dioxide from the air.

4 The plant uses sunshine energy to turn the water and carbon dioxide into its food – sugar.

The plant grows healthily.

▶ *Sunflowers, such as this one, can grow more than 2 metres tall. They grow towards the light, and swivel their huge heads to face the sun.*

What is carbon dioxide?

One of the colourless gases which make up the air on Earth. Other gases in air include nitrogen (about 78%) and oxygen (about 21%).

Why do plants grow towards the light?

Plants grow towards the Sun because they need to take in as much light energy as possible for photosynthesis.

Can a plant see? No. This is lucky because if it did need glasses, it doesn't have a nose or ears to rest them on.

▲ *This worm is burrowing through soil. It breaks up the soil and helps to let the water and air through more easily.*

Is it true that worms help plants grow?

Earthworms do, yes. They pull dead leaves and plants down into the soil. The dead plants rot and leave minerals in the soil which new plants absorb and use for growth and body building.

ALIEN EYE-OPENER

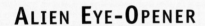

Some plants eat insects. One of the most famous of these is the Venus flytrap. It appears to have lots of large mouths with rows of teeth. But when a fly is caught, it isn't swallowed. It is absorbed into the plant.

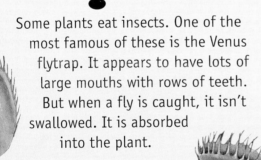

Can plants become ill? Oh yes. They can catch diseases and be attacked by insects. Some sick plants even come out in spots!

Why do birds have feathers?

For lots of reasons. Fluffed up feathers help birds to keep warm. Oiled feathers keep water out. Feathers are light and birds need to be light to fly. Birds move their feathers to change the shape of their wings. This helps them to do different things such as taking off and gliding.

Can all birds fly?

There are over 8650 different types of bird on Earth and most of them can fly, but not all. Penguins can't fly or run very fast, but they are brilliant swimmers.

▶ *This is a swift. Swifts can do everything, from eating and drinking to sleeping, while up in the air.*

A swift can fly up to half a million kilometres a year.

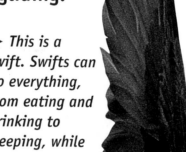

◀ *This is an ostrich. It is 2.5m tall. Ostriches can't fly but they can run very fast indeed. It's hardly surprising with legs this long.*

So, all animals that can fly are birds?

No. Birds are the only animals with feathers, but they are not the only animals who can fly. Insects and creatures called bats can fly. Bats are covered in fur and have warm blood. Bats are **mammals**, not birds.

What are feathers made of?

Feathers are made of **keratin**, which is what human hair and skin are made up of. Every bird has three main types of feathers, each with a different job to do. These are wing feathers, tail feathers and body feathers. Birds lose old feathers and grow new ones. This is moulting.

wing feathers lift the bird upwards and let it fly where it wants to

body feathers are the smallest feathers on this bird. They can fluff up to keep it warm

tail feathers also help in flight

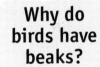

Why do birds have beaks?

Beaks are very useful for catching food. Birds also use their beaks to look after their feathers. The beak is an ideal tool for this. Pulling each feather through the beak to clean it is called preening.

Do birds have arms?

No, usually just two wings and two legs. Wing feathers are made up of primary and secondary feathers. Primary feathers help the bird move forwards and give control when flying. Secondary feathers give the wing a special shape, called an aerofoil, which helps to lift the bird upwards.

◄ *Not all birds' beaks look the same. This macaw has a large sharp beak which is very good for cracking nuts and eating fruit. Birds that eat insects usually have much smaller beaks.*

Why don't fish have fingers?

Fish live underwater. Saltwater fish live in seas and oceans, and freshwater fish live in lakes, rivers and streams. Their fins are for helping them to swim through water. They use their mouths for picking things up. Fish don't *need* fingers.

▲ *The spines on this zebrafish are very poisonous. When the fish feels threatened, it raises the spines as a warning to keep away. The poison is powerful enough to kill a human.*

So fins are just for swimming?

Er, no. Fins are also used by some fish to **vibrate** the water as a warning to other fish to keep away. Some fish use their fins as weapons.

Can fins be used for fighting?

Sometimes. Fish may not have fingers, but some fish fins can give you a nasty prod. Zebrafish even have spiky fins with poison in them.

What else do fish use their fins for?

Some use their fins to say 'choose me!' when looking for a **mate**. For example, the male guppy swims around the female. He fans out his fins to show her what a fine fish he is.

But fish don't shake hands?

How can they, when they don't have hands? Some underwater animals do seem to greet one another, though. When two starfish meet, they often raise an arm to each other. But starfish aren't really fish.

You mean not all underwater animals are fish?

Exactly. The biggest creatures in the seas and oceans are whales, and they are mammals (like humans). Then there are octopuses, **crustaceans** and all sorts of other different types.

▲ *This is a long-finned pilot whale. There are nearly 80 different types of whale. The biggest whale, the blue whale, is the largest mammal on Earth today.*

How can fish live underwater?

Because they don't need to breathe air. Like land animals, fish need oxygen to survive. Unlike land animals, they take their oxygen from water and not air. Water contains **dissolved** oxygen and other gases. Fish have special **organs** called gills to take the dissolved oxygen from water.

A BONY FISH

There are more than 20 000 different **species** of bony fish. Most of them are covered in scales. The scales release a special slime that helps them swim through the water.

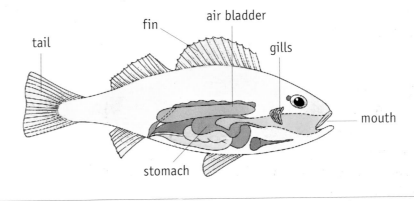

Why don't all animals lay eggs?

Good question. I suppose the simple answer is 'why should they?' There are so many different kinds of animals, it's hardly surprising that they don't all have their young the same way.

Is it only birds that lay eggs?

No. Fish, spiders, **molluscs**, insects and crustaceans lay eggs. Some reptiles also lay eggs, including crocodiles and some snakes. Other snakes give birth to live young.

▲ *The duckbilled platypus is an incredible beast. It is warm-blooded and has fur like a mammal, but it also has webbed feet and a beak-shaped mouth like a duck. It is an excellent underwater swimmer.*

What are 'live young'?

Baby creatures that do not hatch from eggs. Instead, they are born alive. But even a creature that is born live starts off as a single cell, called an egg, *inside* its mother.

But mammals don't lay eggs?

No. Well, yes. In fact there are two – but only two – types of egg-laying mammals: the echidna and the duckbilled platypus. All other baby mammals grow inside their mothers and are born as live young. The time when the baby is growing inside the female is called the gestation period.

◄ *This baby crocodile is about to see the world outside its egg for the first time.*

How long is the gestation period?

It depends on the type of animal. With an American opossum it's 12 days. With humans, it's nine months. This sounds a long time, but with some elephants it's over 23 months. That's almost two years!

ALIEN EYE OPENERS

●

Some baby animals, such as rabbits, are born helpless, blind and without fur. Others, such as hares, are born with thick fur and their eyes open, ready to face the world.

●

Baby hares are born in the open and need to be on the look-out at once. Baby rabbits are born in the safety of a nice warm burrow.

Do all animals care for their young?

No. Some, such as baby turtles, are left to fend for themselves the moment they hatch. Other youngsters, such as apes and elephants, live with their parents for years. Surinam toads carry their young around in pouches on their backs.

► *A bird called a cuckoo fosters out its eggs before they've even hatched. It puts them in other birds' nests. The other birds bring up the cuckoos, thinking they are their own chicks.*

Do families stick together?

It depends on the type of animal. Termites live in colonies of more than a million. Baboons live in troops of up to 200. Elephants live in herds of about 50. Animals such as leopards live and hunt alone.

► *This baby elephant is being cared for by its aunts in the herd.*

How do plants get about?

Unlike animals, most plants grow in one place and stay there. A few plants do travel around, such as the 'tumbleweed', but not under their own power. They are blown by the wind. Plants do manage to get their seeds spread about, though.

What is pollen?

Specks of golden dust found between the petals of flowers, on the stamens. The pollen on some plants is sticky. This is so that it will stick to visiting birds and insects who will then carry it to other plants, making seeds grow. This is called pollination.

◄ These seeds have fallen from a sycamore tree. The 'wings' on the seed case are designed to carry the seeds through the air. They look like tiny helicopters as they spin downwards.

What are seeds?

They are like a plant's eggs which can grow into new plants. Plants only grow seeds when the **pollen** from one plant lands on the stigma of another plant of the same species. When the seeds are ripe, they are ready to move away and to grow.

INSIDE A FLOWER

Pollen lands on the stigma of the flower. The pollen travels into the ovule. The seeds are now pollinated and can begin to grow.

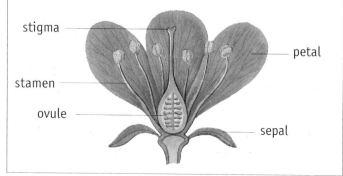

stigma

petal

stamen

ovule

sepal

How do seeds move away?

In lots of different ways. Some plants spread their seeds by releasing them into the wind. Others grow fruit, containing their seeds, which are then eaten by insects, birds and mammals. The animals move on. The seeds pass through their guts and come out, and grow in new places.

◄ *One way for a fungus to spread its spores is by firing them into the air. What looks like smoke in this picture is, in fact, spores that have been fired from this puffball, like pellets from a gun.*

Do humans eat seeds?

Plenty of them. Fruits such as apples, oranges, pears and grapes all contain pips which are fruit seeds. Beans, peas and the pips inside tomatoes are plant seeds. Sunflower seeds are used to make margarine or sunflower oil which is used for cooking. Rice, wheat and nuts are all seeds that are eaten by humans.

◄ *The yellow dots on the outside of this strawberry are seeds. Like many fruits, strawberries are brightly coloured to attract animals.*

You mean some plants *want* to be eaten?

Yes and no. Plants don't have brains, so they can't want anything. For some plant varieties to survive, it is very useful for the plant if its fruit is eaten. That way its seeds spread.

Why can't all the seeds simply fall to the ground and grow there?

Because, in a short time, there would be no room for the new plants to grow. Some plants have pods which contain their seeds. The pods explode to throw the seeds as far as possible.

ALIEN EYE-OPENER

●

Animals can carry seeds off in another way. Some plants grow seeds with special sticky hairs or hooks. These are called burs. Burs get caught in the fur of an animal brushing against them. Once the bur is cleaned off by the animal, it grows into a new plant.

Why do zebras have stripes?

The patterns, shapes and colours that help animals to blend in with their surroundings are called camouflage. They disguise hunters and protect prey.

The stripes confuse any animals that hunt zebras for food. They make the zebra's body look like patches of shadow and light. Zebra stripes are just one example of animal camouflage.

▲ *A zebra and its stripes. The stripes appear to 'break up' the body, so that it isn't one large target for a hunting animal to attack.*

Unlike this zebra's stripes, a tiger has stripes to help it sneak up on animals without being noticed. A leopard has spots for the same reason.

How can an animal's shape be good camouflage?

The shape can make an animal look like something it isn't. A crocodile sitting in a river can look like a floating log. The most incredible examples of this kind of camouflage can be found among insects. A leaf insect looks – you guessed it – just like a leaf, and a stick insect looks like a stick.

▲ *Can you spot the stick insect hiding somewhere in this photograph?*

Are all animals coloured to fit in with the background?

No. It's true that animals such as polar bears are white to match the snow and sharks are bluey-grey to match the sea, but some animals are very brightly-coloured so that they stand out.

But why should an animal want to be seen?

Some animals give out a warning. Brightly-coloured snakes and insects are often poisonous. Their colours are a message to other animals, and the message is: 'Keep away! I am dangerous.'

Could other animals *pretend* to be dangerous by being brightly-coloured?

Good thinking! There are some harmless animals which have both colours and patterns that make them look similar to dangerous animals. For example, there are some harmless insects that look very like wasps.

ALIEN EYE-OPENER

Some plants aren't what they seem. This plant has petals that look like a bee. Real bees come to see what they are. The real bees carry pollen away when they fly off.

◄ *This wasp is black and yellow. Once a creature has tried to eat a wasp and has been stung, it will remember to keep away from black and yellow insects.*

milk snake

◄ *This is a coral snake. It is very, very poisonous. Next to it is a harmless milk snake. It looks like a coral snake so its enemies leave it alone.*

coral snake

17

Why are some living things poisonous?

▼ *This is an Arabian cobra. It is very dangerous. As with all cobras, its fangs are hollow like the needles in syringes. When the snake bites, its fangs fill up with poison called* venom.

In the case of animals, there are two main reasons for being poisonous: *defence* or attack. Some insects are poisonous and taste nasty to put other animals off the idea of eating them. Some snakes use their poison to *paralyse* or kill their prey.

What about poisonous plants and fungi?

They're usually poisonous for defence. An animal will not eat a plant if it has eaten one before that has made it ill.

Can they harm humans?

Oh yes. The berries on some plants could kill us if we ate too many of them. Some fungi, including certain mushrooms and toadstools, are poisonous too. Eating these can make humans very sick indeed.

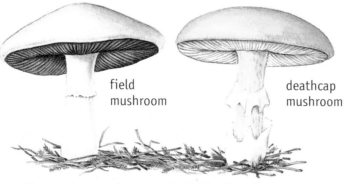

field mushroom

deathcap mushroom

▲ *These two mushrooms look similar, but one of them is harmful. The field mushroom is very tasty. The deathcap mushroom is very poisonous.*

This cobra has its head raised and is ready to strike its prey. Like all cobras, it has a flat hood at the back of its head. The hood makes the cobra look bigger and more frightening.

◄ *This is a laburnum tree. Its seeds are very poisonous. Even the smoke from laburnum burning on a bonfire can make a person very ill.*

How else do some plants defend themselves?

With prickly thorns or stings. These will hurt some animals if they get too close.

◄ *This scorpion can give its victim a nasty sting with its tail. The sting is venom injected into the victim's skin.*

Are all snakes poisonous?

No, don't worry. Less than a third of all snakes are poisonous. That still leaves plenty, though. There are at least six species of cobra alone. The spitting cobra, for example, squirts poison at its victim's eyes.

What other animals use poison to attack?

Mostly insects and spiders. Poisonous spiders have poison in their fangs. A creature called a scorpion has poison in its tail. A scorpion is a close relative of the spider.

ALIEN EYE-OPENERS

●

Some people can 'milk' cobras. 'Milking' means forcing the poison through the fangs and into a jar. This is something that even you shouldn't try, alien!

●

Snakes are reptiles, which means they are **cold-blooded**. They may look slippery, but they are scaly and dry.

Why do birds sing?

For the same reasons that most animals make noises – to claim *territory*, to attract mates, to frighten rivals and to warn of danger. Birds often use an 'alarm call' to warn other birds that danger is close by.

► The woodpecker not only sings to claim its territory, it also sends out its message by tapping its beak on a tree trunk. Hollow tree trunks are best.

► This rosy-patched shrike is marking out its territory by chirping a warning to other birds to keep away.

Do all birds sing the same songs?

No. Don't let them hear you say that! Some birds have very simple songs while other birds, such as the song thrush, sing very complicated melodies.

Like most birds, the rosy-patched shrike can quickly change its song to an alarm call, to warn of danger from a nearby enemy.

What sort of warning noises do other animals make?

Phew, alien. It would take all week to answer this one. Lions roar, cats hiss, dogs growl, gorillas beat their chests... the list is endless. But it's not only noises that animals use to send out 'keep away' messages.

You mean they write threatening letters?

Er, no. Some animals use colours. (Have a look at page 17.) Many animals – from toads to cats – try to make themselves look larger than they really are. Some animals, such as the skunk, give off powerful smells. Lots of animals show off their teeth as a warning to keep away.

ALIEN EYE-OPENER
●
Scientists have taught a few chimpanzees to 'speak' to humans using picture signs or body gestures.

What other messages do animals send out?

Two common ones are 'I've been here' and 'will you be my mate?' A male animal needs to find a female so that they can have young.

But how do underwater animals send messages?

By colour, movement, vibration and sound. When a male stickleback fish is looking for a mate, his tummy turns red. Cuttlefish stroke their mates with their tentacles. Dolphins make lots of different noises. Male humpback whales sing to the females. There are plenty of different ways.

▼ *This Australian frilled lizard throws up its brightly coloured 'collar' when it wants its enemies to stay away. It also opens its mouth wide. The collar makes the lizard look much bigger. The colour makes it look more dangerous.*

◄ *A cat can leave the message 'I've been here' by rubbing a scent gland against something. This leaves behind a special smell.*

Do all plants and animals have blood?

Animals do. Plants don't. But many plants have a thick liquid, called sap, inside them. This sap is so thick that, if the plant is cut, it can appear to bleed. But not all plants have sap.

▶ As with all vertebrates, *the polar bear's blood flows around its body, carrying all the oxygen and food the bear needs to stay alive.*

▼ *This polar bear is warm-blooded but it lives in a very cold climate. As well as its thick coat of white fur, it also has many layers of fat underneath its skin. This helps to keep in its body heat.*

What does sap do?

Sap does a similar job to blood, carrying **nutrients** and minerals around the plant.

▲ *This is a rubber tree. It is being 'bled'. The bark has been cut and the sap is trickling down into a special tray. When left to harden, the sap will become natural rubber.*

But do all animals have blood?

All mammals, birds, reptiles, amphibians and fish have blood. Mammals and birds are warm-blooded. (Humans are mammals, and our healthy blood temperature is 37°C.) Mammals and birds have layers of fat to help keep in the warmth. Reptiles, amphibians and fish are cold-blooded.

So how do reptiles keep warm?

They have to absorb the heat from the outside. This is why reptiles, such as lizards, spend so much time sunning themselves.

ALIEN EYE-OPENER

●

The sap of some trees in rain forests is used as a kind of natural chewing gum by local people.

What happens if they don't keep warm?

They end up doing less and less. That is why snakes and lizards are less active in cold weather.

What about insects?

Yes, they have a type of blood too. A lot of people don't realise this because insect blood is usually colourless, not red like our own.

► *Like all animals, even this tiny insect, the tropical katydid, has a type of blood flowing around its body.*

▲ *This lizard is sunning itself in the baking heat of the desert. When the two feet touching the rock get too hot, the lizard puts down his other two feet, and picks his first two feet off the rock to cool them off.*

What do animals do when they're hungry?

What is a food web?

A group of plants and animals in a habitat where some creatures feed on plants and end up being eaten themselves by meat-eating animals.

Eat plants or eat each other. Life on planet Earth is a never-ending cycle of eating or being eaten. Plants are the basic link in the food webs of life both on land and in water. Animals that only eat plants are called herbivores. Meat-eaters are called carnivores.

◀ *This bat is part of a food web. It has just eaten an insect. Later it may, in turn, be eaten by an owl. The owl also eats insects. Not only that, the owl has insects called* parasites *that live in its feathers and feed off it!*

TYPES OF TEETH

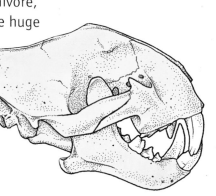

This is the skull of a carnivore, a meat-eater. Look at the huge sharp teeth, which are used for tearing and chewing raw flesh.

This is the skull of a herbivore, a plant-eater. Plant-eaters don't need huge pointed teeth to eat grass and leaves.

What is a habitat?

In this case, a habitat could mean a forest, a lake, a desert, or some other type of surrounding. Each of these habitats has a different food web.

So some types of creature are eaten by creatures that eat the creatures that eat them?

Stop, alien. My head's spinning. If you mean, for example, that a snake will eat an insect and a frog will eat an insect but a snake will also eat a frog, then yes. But some species in a habitat are unlikely to be eaten by anything.

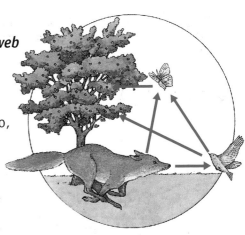

▶ *Part of a forest food web*
1 Insects eat plants.
2 Birds eat insects.
3 Foxes eat birds.
4 But foxes eat insects too, and birds eat plants.

◀ *Part of a lake food web*
1 Plants use light energy.
2 Animal plankton eat plants.
3 Insects eat plankton.
4 Small fish eat water insects.
5 Larger fish eat small fish.
6 Kingfisher eats larger fish.
7 But the larger fish and the kingfisher eat water insects too.

Which animals are unlikely to be eaten?

It depends on the habitat. Usually big, strong carnivores such as lions, tigers and bears. Very few animals dare to attack and eat them. Humans are the safest of them all.

ALIEN EYE-OPENERS

●

An animal that hunts another animal is called a predator. The animal being hunted is called the prey. One animal's predator could be another animal's prey.

●

Large predators often have sharp teeth and claws and huge muscles and paws!

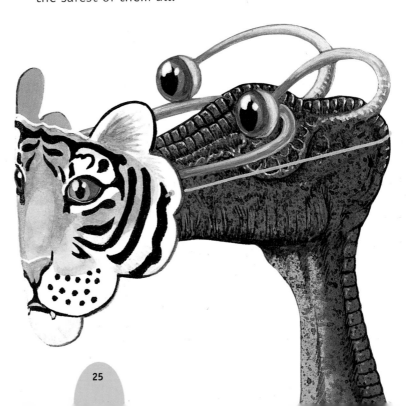

Do animals live in houses?

If you mean do they build houses similar to the ones we live in, no. But many animals do build homes of their own. Some have 'built-in' homes.

◄ *This extraordinary mound is a termite tower. It was built by millions of tiny insects called termites. It is more than 9 metres tall.*

What do you mean 'built-in' homes?

Some animals use a part of themselves as a home! It may sound crazy, but it is true. Animals such as snails, turtles and tortoises have hard shells. They can sleep in them and hide in them for protection.

► *These two pictures are of the same tortoise. In the second picture, it has pulled its head and legs inside the shell to go to sleep.*

► *Over two million termites live in the tunnels inside this tower. They built the tower from soil, spit and animal droppings.*

What about the homes that animals build?

There are so many different kinds. Rabbits live in burrows, beavers live in lodges, wild bees and wasps build nests... the list goes on and on.

I thought birds lived in nests?

Not all the time. Some live in trees, some on the sides of cliffs and some are always on the move. Birds build nests to lay their eggs in and bring up their chicks. A wasp's nest is very different from a bird's nest.

What are these lodges that beavers build?

Piles of sticks, stones and mud. Beavers use their huge front teeth to chew down trees and branches to build dams. Dams are piles of logs across a stream or river which trap water to make a pond. Beavers build their lodge homes in these ponds.

◄ These wasps have built their nest under the eaves of a house.

ALIEN EYE-OPENER

One of the most amazing animal homes is a honey bee's nest. The main part of the nest is the honeycomb. It is made up of hundreds of wax cells where the bees store their honey, which is made from plant **nectar**. Some bees live in **beehives** built by humans.

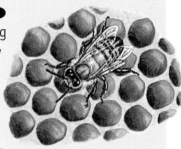

Are all burrows the same?

Certainly not. For example, rabbit burrows are called warrens and are different from badger burrows which are called sets. Each species builds a burrow which is best suited for its way of life.

Do families live together?

Some types of animal live alone. Others live in families. Others live together in their thousands, such as ants and termites.

Not all animals make their own homes do they?

No. Some animals sleep on their feet, or curl up wherever they find natural shelter – under trees or in caves, for example. Some animals, such as bats, sleep in large groups for safety and to keep warm.

▲ This American beaver is building a dam to make a pond. It will build its lodge in the new pond.

How do different animals live together?

▼ A hermit crab scuttles across the seabed with an anemone on its shell.

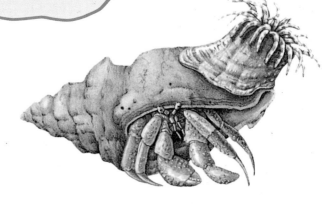

Predators usually only kill what they need to eat. Though most animals need to be on the look-out for trouble, they are not under attack all the time. There are some amazing examples of different species of animals helping each other.

How do different types of animal help each other?

In many different ways. For example, the hermit crab lives in an old sea snail or whelk shell, carrying it around on its back. When the crab moves in, it often invites a poisonous sea anemone to fix itself to the outside of the shell.

◄ *One of the most amazing partnerships in the insect world is shared between the ant and the aphid. This ant is 'milking' one of the aphids kept in the ant hill. The aphid is like a living drinks machine. In return the aphids are protected from predators by the ants.*

But how are they helping each other?

The hermit crab is protected from its predators by the anemone. The anemone, meanwhile, has a free ride with the crab. As it moves around, it has a wider choice of food.

Do they stay friends?

I don't know about that, but when the hermit crab grows larger, it finds a bigger shell and the anemone moves house too.

▲ *The insects that burrow into the buffalo's back could make the buffalo very unhealthy. The oxpecker eats the insects and keeps the buffalo healthy.*

ALIEN EYE-OPENER

●

An incredible example of mammal, fungus and insect helping each other is the badger, the stinkhorn and the fly. If a badger dies, the smell of the rotting carcass may attract enemies to the set. Stinkhorn fungi grow nearby and their powerful smell attracts flies. The flies eat the rotting badger carcass.

Amazing. Any other examples like that?

Probably not quite so incredible, but there is a kind of bird called an oxpecker.

And oxpeckers peck oxes?

The word is 'oxen', and the answer is 'sort of'. The oxpecker uses its beak to dig the harmful insects from the hides of wild cattle such as the water buffalo. This way, the bird has a ready-made meal and the buffalo has its insect pests taken away.

What about fish?

There are a number of types of fish which are cleaned by other, smaller fish. A good example is the butterfly fish and the goatfish. A goatfish lowers its head and changes colour to show that it is ready to be cleaned. The butterfly fish then eats away small **organisms** that are stuck to the goatfish.

▼ *This butterfly fish is eating tiny organisms off the larger goatfish.*

This way the butterfly fish has a free meal and the goatfish is cleaned.

29

Here is a chart of life on Earth

This chart shows the life on our planet divided into ten groups. Each group is shown as a slice of the whole chart. Each slice contains just a few examples of the animals or plants that can be found in that group.

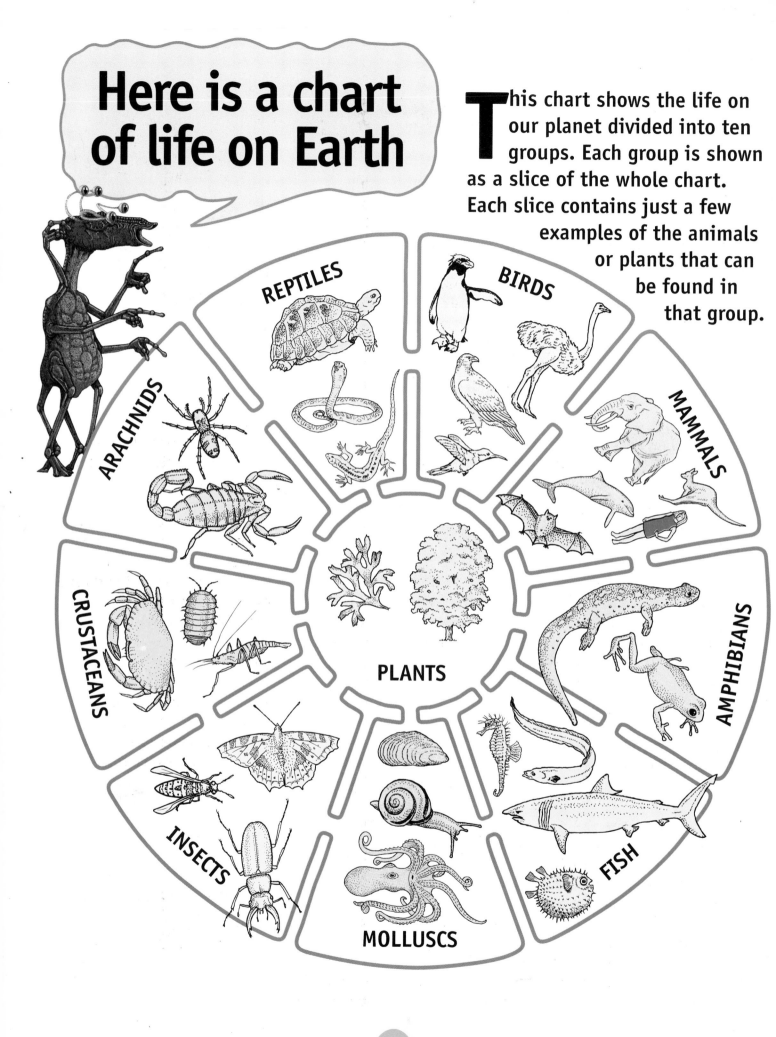

REPTILES

BIRDS

MAMMALS

ARACHNIDS

AMPHIBIANS

CRUSTACEANS

PLANTS

FISH

INSECTS

MOLLUSCS

Glossary

Absorb to take in. For example: a sponge absorbs water.

Aphids a group of tiny insects that suck the juices of plants. For example, a greenfly is an aphid.

Beehives large boxes, built as homes for bees by humans, so the bees' honey can be collected.

Carbon dioxide a gas which is breathed out by people and plants.

Cold-blooded animals, such as fish and reptiles, whose body temperature changes with the temperature that surrounds them.

Crustaceans types of invertebrates, usually with shells and legs, such as lobsters, crabs and woodlice.

Defence to protect from harm.

Dissolve to break up and disappear in water.

Fungi (singular **fungus**) a group of organisms that have no roots, no flowers and no leaves. Fungi feed on dead and decaying organisms. Mushrooms and toadstools are examples of fungi.

Gas a substance which has no shape of its own but which flows and can change shape. Most gases are invisible.

Invertebrates animals without backbones.

Keratin a protein that makes up feathers, hair, claws and horns.

Mammals animals that feed their young with their own milk. All mammals, from humans to dolphins, are warm-blooded.

Mate an animal's partner for breeding.

Molluscs animals with no backbone and a soft body, such as snails and oysters. They are usually protected by a shell.

Nectar the sweet liquid collected from flowers by bees to make honey.

Nutrients anything that gives an animal or plant the nourishment to help it live and grow.

Organism an animal, plant or any other living thing.

Organs parts of an animal's body, such as the heart or the liver, that do special jobs. If an animal's organs don't work properly, the animal will die.

Paralyse to make an animal lose its ability to move.

Parasite an animal or plant that lives on or inside another animal or plant, causing it harm.

Photosynthesis the chemical process which green plants use to make their food from water, carbon dioxide and the sun's energy.

Pollen tiny grains of male cells which are released by flowers. When these land on the female stigma of another plant of the same species, its seeds can grow into new plants. This is how flowering plants reproduce.

Species a group of living things that can breed with each other (but not with any other living things) and which look similar. For example, a lion is a species of mammal. A tiger is another species.

Spores reproductive cells produced by mosses, ferns and fungi. For example, a mushroom spore will grow into a new mushroom.

Territory an area in which an animal lives and feeds and which it defends from other animals.

Venom poison made by animals, such as snakes and spiders.

Vertebrates animals with backbones, such as humans, whales and birds.

Vibrate rapid shaking.

Warm-blooded animals, such as mammals and birds whose body temperature stays about the same, whatever the temperature around them.

I'll be back soon. Perhaps I'll bring a friend.

Index